WD

HOLLYWOOD & GOD

PHOENIX POETS

HOLLYWOOD & GOD ROBERT POLITO

THE UNIVERSITY OF CHICAGO PRESS *Chicago and London*

ROBERT POLITO is the founder and director of the Graduate
Program in Creative Writing and chair of the Writing Program
at The New School. He is the author of four books, including
Savage Art: A Biography of Jim Thompson (1995), winner of the
National Book Critics Circle Award for biography and the
Edgar Award in Criticism of the Mystery Writers of America.
He is also the editor of six books, including the Library of
America's two volumes of crime novels, *American Noir of the
1930s and 1940s* and *American Noir of the 1950s* (1996). His first
book of poems, *Doubles* (1995), was published in the Phoenix
Poets series by the University of Chicago Press.

The University of Chicago Press, Chicago 60637
The University of Chicago Press, Ltd., London
© 2009 by The University of Chicago
All rights reserved. Published 2009
Printed in the United States of America
18 17 16 15 14 13 12 11 10 09   1 2 3 4 5

ISBN-13: 978-0-226-67339-4 (cloth)
ISBN-10: 0-226-67339-1 (cloth)

Library of Congress Cataloging-in-Publication Data
Polito, Robert, 1951–
    Hollywood & God / Robert Polito.
        p. cm. — (Phoenix poets)
    ISBN-13: 978-0-226-67339-4 (alk. paper)
    ISBN-10: 0-226-67339-1 (alk. paper)
    I. Title. II. Title: Hollywood and God.
    PS3566.O474H65   2009
    811'.54—dc22   2008009090

for Kristine

The most confusing situation is to be a ghost who sees terrible things and can't report it.

—FANNY HOWE

Contents

Acknowledgments

Some of these poems were first published, sometimes in different form, as follows:

Agni: "Hollywood Hills" (vol. 58), "Shooting Star" (vol. 58), and "Three Horse Operas" (vol. 58)
Bald Ego: "Pacific Coast Highway" and "Deep Deuce"
Black Clock: "Shame," "Paris Hilton Calls on Jesus," and "Confidential"
Bomb: "Overheard in the Love Hotel"
The Literary Review: "Two or Three Dreams About . . ." (vol. 45, no. 3, Spring 2002)
Mississippi Review: "New York School"
Open City: "Please Refrain From Talking During The Movie"

"The Great Awakening" was first published in *Shakespeare Yearbook: Shakespeare After 9/11*, edited by Douglas A. Brooks and Matthew Biberman.
"Barbara Payton: A Memoir" was first published in *O.K. You Mugs*, edited by Luc Sante and Melissa Pierson (New York: Pantheon Books, 1999).
"Last Seen" was first published in *110 Stories: New York Writers After September 11*, edited by Ulrich Baer (New York: New York University Press, 2004).

Grateful acknowledgment is made to the editors of all these publications.

"The Harrowing of Dorchester" is for Lisa.

HOLLYWOOD & GOD

Hollywood Hills

Her soul drifts across the continent.
She keeps returning to the hills above Hollywood

The famous addict who once made love to her,
after watching her first with another woman.

She is remembering the night he mocked her
for crying out his name,

I was your own private whore.

Still damp from the shower, still almost
naked, but not yet of guile,

He is telling the love-sick woman what he guesses
she refuses to hear,
things are bad, how can he not leave?

But as a rose turns and closes

The next morning he thinks he overhears the hotel staff moan
his name—name in the night she repeated so passionately—with derision.

* * *

In the running ink of the rain-soaked newspaper,
she glimpses the forecast: rain.

My life was difficult for lots of reasons

Before I was an actress I worked at the trendy New York hotel,
he kept trying to get me up to his room—this was before
I really met him—
but I always said no.

Even though she tells him it makes her feel coarse,
she amuses him with stories of her ancient lovers.
You will never get over this being an actress, he says.
The scratched disc stuck on *love you love you love*

* * *

She phones his machine, demanding no more calls,
forgive me, I can't talk to you, talking
to you makes me phone other people, one in particular, to ask
him to stop calling too, and this must stop.

Like a singer who ghosts his own voice for the live show

There were always three of us in bed
him, whatever girl he really wanted, and me
sucking away—

I wondered, she says, how God would remake me.
Now I know.

Barbara Payton: A Memoir

For a few years during the early 1960s my father tended bar at the Coach and Horses on Sunset, in Hollywood. Weekdays he inventoried the sale of stamps, money orders, and Pitney Bowes Machines as supervisor of a Santa Ana post office, close to where he lived in a tidy dingbat studio. But I was about to turn thirteen, and he hoped to send me to a "real college." The post office discouraged second jobs for government employees of his rank, so my father moonlighted only at bars, all transactions cash.

The Coach and Horses lured patrons with the natty coat of arms of a British pub, but inside the landscape registered saloon. This was residential Hollywood. Cocktail lounges unattached to hotels or eateries still tended to be rare in Los Angeles, and survived on local drunks who could swing the tab—wall drinks sixty-five cents. Fourteen stools along a runty bar, half as many booths strung in a miniature railroad, the vibes at the Coach and Horses read dark: dusky paneling, blackout drapes, shaded lamps. Haul in a couple of slot machines and you might feel transported to Vegas, even Barstow.

The summer of 1962 my father let me join him for his Saturday stints. My parents already were separated, and he took custody of me weekends. In the beginning I was too shy to connect with anyone but him, but I loved the overheard chatter, wisecracks, complaints, the provocative fragments of confessions. The silent drinkers, draining the day over the *Citizen-News*, I also admired, because they were harder to figure out. I read novels and music magazines sitting at a desk in the ruins of an office the staff tagged the "Black Hole of Calcutta," up a shaky flight of stairs at the back; or sometimes I moved to the last booth, where we covertly replaced the mood lighting with a forty-watt bulb—still too dim to menace the perpetual twilight. We made a day of it, before heading off to supper and a movie. The whole experience was a lot like going to a loud library.

We were about three or four weeks into our routine when a day manager, probably Rodney, an occasional DJ at Hollywood High dances, started to lecture my father. He felt sorry for me, he said, rotting away doing nothing on another beautiful LA afternoon. His concern could also have betrayed the sodden departure the previous night of his latest barback—a fiftyish ex-race car driver fleeing overdue alimony. (The Coach and Horses rotated help nearly every payday.)

Rodney suggested I could better occupy myself. For exactly a dollar less than minimum wage, he put me to work retrieving bottles and splits, sweeping cigarettes off the black and red carpeting, soaking glasses. My father and I opened the bar Saturdays at noon. Quickly I graduated also to Friday evenings.

I was too thrilled to tell my mother about my secret employment, but lied cautiously.

Ralph and Leo from Holloway House stopped at the Coach and Horses evenings after work, and Leo usually returned Saturday. Back then, Holloway House—situated up on Holloway Drive—published bottom-feeder Hollywood autobiographies along the lines of *Jayne Mansfield's Wild, Wild World*. Earnestly sensational scientific exposes, such as *Psychodynamics of Unconventional Sex Behavior* by Paul J. Gillette, Ph.D., and unexpurgated classics, *Satyricon: Memoirs of a Lusty Roman*, rounded off the list.

Leo was an old columnist for the *Hollywood Reporter*, a squat, mischievous man. He would discover me with a book at the bar during the ordinarily vacant afternoons, and he started to joke with me about school. Leo could talk to anyone.

One day he arrived lugging a fat brick of loose pages—"What's your spelling like?" he quizzed me. His company needed a person to fix galleys. Leo said he was sick of doing everything himself. For exactly a dollar more than minimum wage I signed on as the exclusive proofreader at Holloway House.

This was perfect, since I would now be paid double for reading at the Coach and Horses. The first titles I remember were *Hollywood Screwballs* and *The Many Loves of Casanova*.

The Coach and Horses swirled with legends of famous lushes who boozed there—Hitchcock, Jason Robards, Richard Harris, William Holden. But the only star—if star's the right name for her—we ever saw was Barbara Payton.

Someone, no doubt Leo, told me about "the scandal." Back in the early 1950s Payton was coming off a leading role in *Kiss Tomorrow Goodbye* when she met B-movie actor Tom Neal at a party. Within days she ended a relationship with Franchot Tone, proclaiming her engagement to Neal. But believing marriage to the more prominent and accomplished Tone might advance her Hollywood stature, Payton ditched Neal—only to return again. "He had a chemical buzz for me that sent red peppers down my thighs," she subsequently explained to *Confidential*. But the night before Payton was to marry Neal, she contrived a date with Tone. Neal waited up for them. The former boxer smashed Tone's nose, and sent him to the hospital with a concussion and fractured cheekbones. Tone secretly underwent plastic surgery.

Payton wed Tone upon his recovery. She divorced him fifty-three days later. Neal and Payton toured in a backwater road production of *The Postman Always Rings Twice*, but both careers derailed.

Connecting *that* Barbara Payton to the woman in the Coach and Horses demanded impossible time travel. Our Barbara Payton oozed alcohol even before she ordered a drink. Her eyebrows didn't match her brassy hair; her face displayed a perpetual sunburn, a map of veins by her nose. Her feet swelled, and she carried an old man's potbelly that sloshed faintly when she moved. Her gowns and dresses looked more like antique costumes than clothes, creased and spotted. She must have weighed two hundred pounds.

She didn't resemble anyone two actors would fight over.

Barbara Payton was then thirty-four years old—younger than my father. She didn't come across as bitter, or angry, or crazy. She clearly wasn't rich, but she always carried ten or twenty dollars for her drinks.

Beyond the rosé, Barbara emanated a chronic self-abdication that outmaneuvered most humiliations. If a new customer of the Coach and Horses wondered whether there might be any regrets, she'd pause, taste her wine, and answer as though she had never considered the question. "You know if I had to do it all over again, I'd do the same. It's all in heaven in a little black book with neat lines. You are what you are and there's no out. You do what you have to do."

She was the first person I met who spoke like she lived in a movie. She conversed through hard-boiled maxims.

"I got news for you baby—nobody's civilized. You peel off a little skin and you got raw flesh."

"But forever is just a weekend—more or less."

She had a theory different sleeping pills will give you different sorts of dreams. She couldn't recall any brand names—only colors: red for passionate dreams, white for horror dreams. Barbara maintained she told this to Gregory Peck while they were filming *Only the Valiant*. He jotted it down.

She enjoyed washing men's dirty shirts—said she liked it the way someone liked playing golf.

Barbara entered the Coach and Horses every Saturday afternoon at five o'clock, and she left at seven, as methodical as a stopwatch conductor. Fridays she would land around eleven and remain on her stool until we closed at one. Leo sometimes would escort Barbara home—Friday, anyway, but never Saturday, when she always insisted on leaving alone. Her apartment, it turned out, was right on Holloway Drive.

Ralph once joked that Leo could smell a book in a Hollywood toilet. Soon after my proofreading chores started for Holloway House, Leo advanced Barbara Payton $250 for her life story.

He loaned her a tape recorder to reconstruct her memories. A young woman Leo knew named Nancy—I heard later she dated, maybe even married one of the Wilsons, of the Beach Boys—would actually write the text. My job was to transcribe the tapes.

Leo titled Barbara's story after a line she regularly used around the bar: *I Am Not Ashamed*.

I typed on a sleek Remington Portable (courtesy of Holloway House) up in the "Black Hole of Calcutta." Barbara's tapes came as a revelation—to me, though hardly, I suspect, to Leo and Ralph. If her Hollywood past loomed a distant mystery, her present amounted to an "other life." Five minutes into the first reel Barbara was describing her practices as a hooker along the Sunset Strip.

On the tapes she compared her book to "a kind of detective story. I—or we—want to find out what happened that started me on the skids, down, down, down, down." Yet Barbara was short.on motive or responsibility. Even "the scandal" seemed less a life-transforming watershed than another spongy anecdote.

Barbara herself charted her fall as an inverse pyramid of declining cash. There was stardom, and $10,000 a week. Then, all but inexplicably, no roles—instead $300 "gifts" tactfully deposited inside her purse by producers. Then, $100 gifts, left less discreetly on her dresser. She bounced a check at a Hollywood grocery store to purchase liquor. She slept with her landlady's husband for the rent, and on Christmas Eve with an actor friend for $50, then $20 Johns, then $10.

Now—her voice woozed from the speaker—"The little money I accumulate comes from old residuals, poetry, and favors to men. . . . I love the Negro race and I will accept money only from Negroes. . . . White men don't seem to go for me anymore. . . . Wine and bare bodies and nightmare sleep and money that was never enough to pay the bills. . . . One night I realized I was in bed with a Negro. He was gentle and kind to me. . . . He gave me five dollars . . . five dollars!"

The hooking explained Barbara's meticulous timetable in the Coach and Horses. Friday she drank after she roused a few bucks. Saturday she braced herself against the evening ahead.

The poems, though, appeared to scratch a revenant of pride amid the drift. "I decided it was alright to be a hustler as long as I wrote poetry," Barbara declared on the tapes. "Even in bed with a trick I could think of lines." Her poems zigzagged like her stories—the few poems she showed us. Fragments, essentially: some phrases about Tom Neal, followed by an image from her Texas childhood, ending on a hymn to rosé wine. A writer friend, she mentioned, sold them to a "way-out Beatnik journal" for her.

I asked my father if he knew about Barbara's secret. He laughed. Anything she did was OK, he said, assuming she didn't do it in the Coach and Horses—and provided she stayed away from me.

He did allow Barbara to take me to the movies, twice, each occasion one of her old films. While we were working on the book, *Kiss Tomorrow Goodbye* played at the Oriental, a few doors down Sunset. Another afternoon we rode the bus over to the Encore at Melrose and Van Ness for *Trapped*.

Watching seated alongside Barbara, I was startled by her glamour—slim, blonde, beautiful—and the strangeness of actually knowing someone who made movies.

Seeing those films again, and some others for this history, I'm struck more by her obvious disquiet as an actress. Barbara Payton starred in roughly eleven features between 1949 and 1955, but she flashes anxiously from the margins of her movies. Her presence is fleeting—even when she attained top billing for *Only the Valiant* or *Bride of the Gorilla* her on-screen time amounted to staggered cameos; her command of role is hesitant, uneasy. As Holiday Carleton in *Kiss Tomorrow Goodbye* Payton wobbles from ingenue to she-devil. When facing into the camera she scarcely moves, except her mouth to deliver her lines. Her transitions roll as a succession of production stills, a flip book of faltering moods.

She does not so much inhabit a character as impersonate a starlet—an act, I suppose, she merely extended to the Coach and Horses, or the Sunset Strip. In her movies Payton is a doll dropped into a scene to insinuate sex. Directors took to filming her from the side, her breasts vaulted in silhouette.

Only Edgar Ulmer understood how to spin her anxiety into an advantage. For *Murder Is My Beat*—Payton's last film—he cast her as Eden Lane, a nightclub singer convicted of murder. On the way to prison Lane is convinced she sees the supposed victim from her train, and escapes. For much of the action the viewer is uncertain whether Lane committed a crime. Payton's tension plays as suspense, her hesitations as possible instability, an intimation that she might indeed be a murderess.

On the tapes Barbara asserted she bankrolled the completion of *Murder Is My Beat* by sleeping with a prosperous stockbroker. "Mr. Shellout" she christened him.

She even put me—or someone like me—into the book. "One night when a friend brought over another friend," she suggested, "and the first one left leaving me with this kid. . . . He was so awed by me I went to bed with him and then wouldn't take his money. That's how lousy a hooker I was."

This never happened. But many of Barbara's implausible stories weren't so readily dispelled. She also clutched secrets—her first husband, their son in Texas.

Nancy and I probed, and verified what we could; then we camouflaged the rest against lawsuits. The whole process took us about a month.

* * *

I Am Not Ashamed finally appeared in 1963. When Barbara Stanwyck read Payton's autobiography, she apparently quipped, "Well, she damn well should have been!"

Tom Neal married, and his wife died of cancer. He remarried, and opened a landscape business in Palm Springs. During a domestic dispute his new wife was shot to death. Like his character Al Roberts at the conclusion of Edgar Ulmer's film *Detour*, Neal maintained the killing was an accident. Barbara attended the trial wearing dark glasses. Neal served six years in the California Institute for Men at Chino before being paroled.

On her way back from Mexico in 1967, Barbara Payton died of complications from alcoholism in the bathroom of her parents' San Diego home. "A blonde movie actress in Mexico," she once said, "is always cause for celebration."

My parents divorced, and my mother never discovered the Coach and Horses. But my father sent me as far east from the bar as possible—to Catholic Boston College. By then he had moved on to the more upscale Firefly Lounge.

Holloway House discovered Iceberg Slim, and everything changed.

Paris Hilton Calls on Jesus

My God makes me feel good.

There is a grandeur and purity in all I see.

A grandeur and purity around and in me.

Now that I'm grown up, back
to Jesus is like back to the cool bars.

I used to love popping E and dancing all night
in clubs with the boy I married—
                                    & divorced.

At a party you can always count on him
to chat up the skankiest girl in the room.

Not me, of course.
—Not that I'm better than anyone else.
You have to be humble:
I'll go skinny-dipping with you, pal, but
I won't sleep with you,
if you know what I mean.

Ectasy makes you feel so close—
but we weren't close.
You could almost blame my whole marriage on E.

I can only meditate when I wear earmuffs,
the kind you'd find at a gun range.
Now when I pray that way,
it's like I'm firing back at the world.

Two or Three Dreams About . . .

1. Detour

a rented house   rainy season
Behind the green wood-paneled wall

       First only on storm nights,
Then every night—
Our family of skunks tries and fails to lift
And fails to lift again
The door into the crawl space;
Door banging down on its hinges each time they fail;

My mother breaks the darkness,
            arriving in the night

Forgive me if I sound theatrical—I hear her say—
But your brother will try to kill himself,
Then try to kill himself again;
That's once for each time he watched me take too many pills,
And wouldn't telephone you or your sister;

Inside the crawl space the skunks screech and mate,
Send their secretions through the heating system;

My mother during her final illness
Filled any gap with the word phlegm:

"I was eating my phlegm when the nurse came in to take my phlegm."

"Please take care of your phlegm,
He'll need you now that I'm phlegm."

Bold behind glass the cats hiss at the skunks,
For all our banging, shouting, nothing—
Still they lift the door and crowd in;

Where did you leave his body?
—Vera surprises Al Roberts in Edgar Ulmer's *Detour*—
This buggy belonged to a fellow named Haskell;

As the cats scratch at the heating grates,
Stretch a claw down to the crawl space.

2. *Grendel's Mother*

My father's earliest memory is
Not the icebox overturning onto him,
But his mother lifting it off;

That was right before she fled alone to New York City;
He told us instead that she died.

The *Beowulf* poet remembered Grendel's mother
As "mournful and ravenous."

In my father's dream
His father is Grendel's mother

Not
     —as once upon a time he feared—

A bully
Backhanding his wife after she cracked a glass of their wedding crystal;

A drunk
Relieving himself on the kitchen floor;

But only a creature in a book.

He dreams the disenchantment of the world.
Not *monster* but paper   ink   bottle   father.

Mike the Winger

City of Presidents,
city of the Granite Railway and Fore River Shipyard.

But city too of condoms ground into our pitcher's rubber,
and city of water rats and black leeches floating in the spring runoff.

City of the first Howard Johnson's, the first Dunkin Donuts,
city of Lee Remick modeling summer dresses for her father's store,

And city now where Beatles albums drop from the sky
as Mike the Winger speaks from inside a circling crowd—

Pockmarked, pimpled and blazing,
he looks, Tommy LeBlanc said, like someone set his face on fire
then stomped it out with golf shoes.

As he straddles his new Black Phantom,
as he rocks on his new red Keds,
as he pounds his wire basket of new LPs,

Mike demonstrates the legendary gesture that gave him his name.

"I play 'em once, then I wing 'em," he says—

Every afternoon Mike spins his own Top 40 from his bike
like a paperboy launching the *Patriot Ledger* across our lawn—

"Those Rolling Stones? Those Beach Boys? Those groups all you kids like?
They're OK. But man, I love them Beatles—
they wing up real good!"

What about his parents? Where does he grab all that cash?
Nobody stops to ask,
caught in the awe of the grander phenomenon—

Manna from heaven—

Records eased from their jackets and arced into air—

Records pristine and gleaming in trees,
records scratched and gritty on the streets,

Amid shouts of *Go Mike, Go nuts, Go wingnut,*
Come on Mikey baby wing one over here—

The hits just keep on coming . . .

The dead are everywhere,
but if Mike is still alive,
he'd be tracking retirement age—

Though how do you retire from something like winging?
Mere technological obsolescence? Mike frustrated by CDs,
casualty to a digital age?

Maybe winging records is like making movies,
or saying Mass,
your calling—

You do it until you can't do it anymore.

Mike worshipped the early Gods of rock 'n' roll,
Chuck Berry, Elvis, Little Richard, and Buddy Holly,
then he winged everybody else.

None of the records Mike tossed have ever gone away.
Who would have guessed that?

City of John Adams and John Quincy Adams, our 2nd & 6th Presidents.

City of Myles Connor, rockabilly singer & art thief.

City of Robert Polito.

City of Mike the Winger.

Please Refrain From Talking During The Movie

When I can't make you understand I repeat myself
I repeat

If you don't stop asking me all these questions how
Will I understand anything

Please refrain from talking during the movie

I need a life that isn't just about needing
To escape my life

Please God please may Carrie please fall for me

I want to show off my hidden camera
I'm an informer but I have my limits

You hurt him once before now what
If she's there I don't know if I can go

Please refrain from talking during the movie

Leave a message if you can't reach me
To exit press enter and don't forget your receipt

When I think I read new things I want
A life where I read and think new things

Please refrain from talking during the movie

I want to know nothing
Again

Please God please may Carrie please fall for me

I repeat myself when I can't
Make you understand I repeat

Overheard in the Love Hotel

after Nan Goldin

Again the cab slips west down 14th almost
To the river—
The cobbled meat market, steel grates down;
A thrown-up Christmas tree
Lot on an old dock beyond the stalled highway;
A whiff of blood and the first snow
That keeps not falling.

We've just checked into the Love Hotel—
Film noir signatures on the register:
"Tom Neal," "Ann Savage";
Spouses discarded, even her
Two other lovers forsaken at the bolted door.

Fading polyester roses drape the bed—matching
Trellis on an overhead mirror; evening breeze
Out of Hoboken through cracked panes
—Nothing can dispel the half-life traces of Roach Bomb
She chases with a blunt cigar . . .
"So sexy you brought these. This is sweet—
And throws a little curve into the day."

Blue ice pail; Absolut from a frosted cup.
Raking her new coil of brassy curls,
"Can you picture me with gray hair?

My mother passed her forties as a blonde;
Now you know my true color—

You and a few others."
Wrapping her ankles around his, she pins
Him on the spread
As from a room upstairs springs rattle to a finish;
"It's like I'm one of them . . .
All the passion, the ecstasy—
We spend the rest of our lives trying to shake."

Reflected along the ceiling, freckles
From her back rotate constellations
He traces like a blind man reading a star map;
"You've got to see who I am—
These yearnings, sometimes they last two years,

Or they can burn out after all of seven seconds;
But they're intense, and very real."
The wall phone rings—*Twenty minutes, please*.
"I wish I could say I didn't know
How they call just before your time's up,
Or not getting your hair wet in the shower,
The towels that irritate your skin"—

Six-inch scar across her panty line
Where last spring the surgeon
Scooped out her insides,
Reddening with soap and steam;
And still stings when she wears silk.

Outside, snow holding. Another cab.
"Where was I, tonight? I've been
Lying to Kevin about Steve, Steve about Kevin;
And to Stanley about both of them . . .
Only you have the whole story.
First time I lie to you—
Then you'll know we're really going someplace."

New York School

a. Larry Rivers

That was the night the fastest talker in New York
Accused me of talking too fast into his message machine.
His anger made him talk even faster.

b. Alice Neel

When my heart broke water,
You could bottle his laughter;
My whirligig lover—
Gurgling with scissors in his back.

c. Delmore Schwartz

That camera's only shooting blanks,
180° of show & tell for the marks.
It's the ones the Rockefellers hide that do their seeking;
Remember: if you can see the Empire State Building,
The Empire State Building can see you.

Three Horse Operas

for Patti Smith

At the end of Bing Crosby's *Riding High* his horse
Will be buried in the clay of the racetrack where he fell,
As a lesson for all of us. Sad, waggish Bing,
The Mob didn't want Broadway Bill to win, so the jockey
Pulled on the reins until the thoroughbred, straining
Over the finish line first, collapsed, heart attack.

I loved you like a guitar string breaking
Under the conviction of a clumsy hand—
Something like that . . . I suppose I must have
Been thinking of you and your complex and beautiful band,
Except the image demands I hold the guitar,
If not you, and the broken string, as

Over and over loudspeakers call riders to the starting gate.
The track bartender and a teller, a sharpshooter and the chess master
Wrestler, the petty con man and a cop, reprise their parts.
The heist gang dons clown masks, and
Sherry will betray George, and Johnny can't love Fay,
And the fortune in the suitcase just blows away.

What a Friend

This is the story your mother told, a bit
Skeptically, as if to show how someone changed.
Your Aunt Barbara says she was driving home from the hospital.
It was raining. It was late. And when she crossed over the bridge,
She got a flat. She pulled the car onto the shoulder, and
Worked the directionals, but no one would stop in the rain.
When she finally got out herself and opened the trunk,
Guess what, there was no jack. A perfectly good spare, but
No jack. Your Uncle Johnny left it in the garage, or something.
That's when it happened. That's when Jesus showed up.
He lifted up the back of the car, and she changed the tire.
That anyway is what your Aunt Barbara's saying now.
I didn't know Catholics could be Pentecostal. Imagine
Jesus Christ traipsing around like that, helping people get home.

Deep Deuce

As phantoms direct life from the shadows,

                                              I feel

I leaned on something,
                and it broke.

My father on the porch with his crosswords said,
this must be what it feels like to be dead;

When I returned from the dead there was no one to greet me,
but still you are glad—

I wander the ruins the way my tongue
wanders my missing teeth,
the bricks and mortar of Deep Deuce
rotted like molars in an ancient mouth;

Here Charlie Christian might have walked—

The astrologer counseled patience
and creative imaging:

       Step One: Visualize
an object that symbolizes the accursed influence. Picture yourself throwing
it into a furnace.

Step two: Visualize
the person who is responsible for the curse. Imagine one end of a rope
is tied around your waist and the other around that person. Picture yourself cutting
the rope with a chainsaw as you call out, "You have no power over me!"

Step three: Repeat
twice a day for eleven days . . .

You visualize her green boots inside the furnace . . .

—No. You are in a crematorium and you see
her perfect and corruptible body on a tray sliding into fire;

Then you see yourself cutting the rope that ties you together with a saw;

And then at last your own imperfect and corruptible body—I mean, me—
calls out

and I jump in after her.

The Harrowing of Dorchester

If they find life on other planets, won't that mean the Bible is wrong? This was the summer after Sputnik, the summer of 1958, and my family was riding back from two weeks in a rented cottage—one of a colony of identical A-frames—near Buzzards Bay, Cape Cod. As he drove our car along the Southeast Expressway past Braintree and Quincy toward Dorchester, my father, who reinforced his aspirations of my growing up a scientist with astronomy charts, a plastic microscope, and a vast chemistry set beyond my six and a half years, shifted the conversation to the Soviet launch of the previous November, space travel, and the possibility of life on other planets.

UFOs were our shared infatuation that year, and I joined in his car talk avidly. But I found myself assaulting him with a question that never occurred to me before.

I don't know if I was confused, or if I wished to test and confuse him. In the front seat, both my parents seemed flummoxed, my mother fidgety, even angry.

Turning his head back from the wheel of the two-tone, secondhand Oldsmobile we had waxed together that morning, my father broke the silence. "Bobby, I guess you're right. . . ."

A few nights later, he revisited our drive home when he was tucking me into bed. My mother wanted him to speak with me. She telephoned the Monsignor, and he told her what I asked in the car didn't disprove the Bible. "God wrote the Bible about earth," he said. "Those beings on other planets could have their own Bibles."

But he sounded only half-convinced.

How candid was my father when he talked to me about God, the Bible, or for that matter UFOs? I never knew what he was thinking, why he went to mass with us every Sunday. I assumed he went to please my mother, and because not going would be too decisive a break, but who can say? After his mother died, when he was five or six, as I understood it, he was on his own, raised by his older sister. That my father was a supervisor in the post office, with a home and a wife and children, all appeared to astonish him. Though presumably he spoke only Italian inside his South End house as a kid, around us he seemed to pride himself on *not* knowing any Italian, pride himself on being an American. I'm not Italian, he said, I'm American. His tone around me sometimes was that of a coconspirator, winking at the dumb rules, and sometimes that of a ghost, carrying rumors of a life beyond our house, cynical and wounded at once. One of his recurrent catchphrases involved the notion that there were three subjects a gentleman never talked about: politics, women, and religion. The Boston Catholics I grew up with during the 1950s and 1960s, the predominantly *Irish* Catholics who inhabited St. Mark's parish, were not people of the Word or the Book. Stiff, greasy from kitchen fumes, our Bible sat on the bottom shelf in a rear hallway under cookbooks and the old electrical engineering and psychology texts my father studied at night school on the GI Bill. From the start I was made to appreciate I would attend the parochial grammar school at St. Mark's, where Sisters of St. Joseph kept academic discipline; after that, if I worked hard, my parents vowed to send me to a good Catholic high school, despite the costs, and on to college. The Bible somehow was related to a race of sinners called Protestants, who, my mother and grandmother said, revolted against the Church and were condemned by God to hell.

Since we didn't know any Protestants, it hardly mattered. Dominated by my mother, and her mother—my Nana—the eyes our family set on the outside world radiated distrust. Ethnic identities sustained an almost occult solidity, and their wariness extended to my Italian American father. Nana could toll any argument to a halt with a reminder he was living in a house her Irish husband paid for. I watched my father twist in his chair at the head of the dining room table during these arguments, or pace the hallway shouting, you know I can always move out, and disappearing outside to work, like paint or rake leaves. If you go, I'll go with you, I'd tag after him. We didn't talk about my father's mother, or his father: they stayed off-limits in a tacit, charged way, and to this day I've never seen a photo of my Italian grandparents. Every afternoon after school my mother would sit down beside me with my homework, for upwards of three or four hours as my friends played stickball in the parking lot behind the grocery store at the corner of our street. Her tone during these sessions at the kitchen table over my schoolbooks seemed to say, "That world out there, it's hard, you're going to need all the help you can get." She never said this exactly, but I always knew what my mother was thinking, though often it was the opposite of what she was saying, even believed she was saying. Beyond my father's random popular science paperbacks, there were no books in our house, no musical recordings, we never went to the movies, rarely traveled out of Boston, and I don't think we owned a TV. If her little scholar's attention wandered through the window and down the street, she yanked it back with a coat hanger she held ready in her right hand. Her connections inside the Sisters of St. Joseph allowed her access to the answer keys the nuns relied on to grade our quizzes, and our preparations together ran months ahead of my class. I was so bored and restless in St. Mark's that eventually the sisters sent me home with a diagnosis that I must have worms.

Our English reader at St. Mark's paraphrased heroic episodes from the life of Christ, but all my other early encounters with the Bible passed through the filter of the Baltimore Catechism, titled for The Third Plenary Council of Baltimore (1884). Every lesson opened with a few lines loosely lifted from the New Testament, but the teachings themselves seemed calculated to relocate young readers as far as possible from the words of Christ and the Gospels. Our first lesson announced the beliefs of the Catholic Church came instead from The Apostle's Creed—a mnemonic formula established at the Council of Trent in 1563, which derived more from Augustine than the Bible. Among the drawings scattered through the catechism, full and empty milk bottles tracked the debasement of pure into sinful souls, and our "Good Shepherd" tended actual sheep on a real farm. A conspicuously European Christ performed his miracles surrounded by his European disciples and, often, a troupe of American school children, our time-transported stand-ins who mingled among the mourners at his crucifixion. For a young *male* reader, the catechism encouraged identification with Christ, portrayed in text and illustration as another white prince from our storybooks. It wasn't hard to make an imaginative connection to this boy who, with his ambiguous relation to his earthly parents, challenged his mother in a Jerusalem temple, as each night after supper I retreated from homework down to the cellar where I kept my own books, toys, experiments, an ancient radio, and hid out until it was time for bed. Unlike Protestant or Jewish friends who might retain forever early inflections of the King James or the Hebrew Bible as a collective interior melody, the enduring tune from my religion lessons pitched insistent questions against pat answers:

1. *Who made us?*
    God made us.
2. *Who is God?*
    God is the Supreme Being who made all things.
3. *Why did God make us?*
    God made us to show forth His Goodness and to share with us His everlasting happiness in heaven.

A few days before my First Holy Communion, my mother surprised me with a small present wrapped in tissue paper and sealed with purple ribbon. Your aunt, she said, put this away for you when she got sick. Opened, the package contained everything I would need to celebrate my First Communion, including a Latin missal inside a leather slipcase and a Rosary strung with heavy onyx beads and a wood cross. My classmates would have to make do with plastic, I noticed, when the nuns called us to a dress rehearsal in St. Mark's Church, where the Sister Superior could inspect our First Communion clothes and kits. As I explained about Sister Mary Dionetta and her present, the Sister Superior smiled—she entered the order with my aunt, she told me, and I must be proud of her now in heaven. But on a closer look at my missal, rubbing the cover and turning the pages inside, she snapped the book shut. She blessed herself, repeated the Our Father, no longer smiling at me.

My missal was *heresy*, she announced to the assembly, I must send your missal into the Archdiocese, she said, where it will be destroyed. The heresy, I learned once I ran home in tears and my mother phoned the school, involved something like this. The Imprimatur who signed off on my missal was Father Leonard Feeney, a recently excommunicated Jesuit priest my aunt served alongside years before, back when they both lived at St. Paul's Church in Cambridge. I visited my aunt at St. Paul's during the months my uncle John was in the VA hospital, and she and the other nuns would take care of me so my mother and grandmother could take care of him. Father Feeney presided over the St. Benedict Center, formerly the Harvard Catholic Club, during the 1940s. Evelyn Waugh, I later discovered, explored the St. Benedict Center on the counsel of Clare Boothe Luce:

> [Father Feeney] fell into a rambling denunciation of all secular learning which became more and more violent. He shouted that Newman had done irreparable damage to the Church then started on Ronnie Knox's *Mass in Slow Motion* saying "To think any innocent girl of 12 could have this blasphemous and obscene book put in her hands" as though it was *Lady Chatterley's Lover.* I asked if he had read it. "I don't have to eat a rotten egg to know it stinks." Then I got rather angry and rebuked him in strong words.

Father Feeney insisted that there was no salvation outside of the Church, declaiming anti-Semitic speeches on Boston Common. But if retrospect could void Father Feeney's Imprimatur, were all the marriages he performed while a priest invalid? All the dying souls he intoned the Last Rites over condemned to hell? Neither my parents nor the other nuns ever logged the Sister Superior's spotty theology. Cardinal Cushing officiated at our First Communion Mass, at once magisterial and elfin in gold vestments, crosier, and red suede boots. The theatrics of the Latin Mass cannot be exaggerated. I recall a Good Friday Passion at the downtown cathedral where the choirs, incense, cloth-draped statues, an agonized Stations of the Cross, and Cardinal Cushing, this time arrayed head to feet in purple, would only be matched thirty years later by a performance of *Aida* inside the Roman Arena at Verona.

A few months after my First Communion, instead of swallowing the host at Sunday Mass, I started secretly passing it from my mouth to a handkerchief for preservation at home in a jar I hid among the powders of my chemistry set. My idea was that reserves of such potent magic could prove useful someday—for or against what I can't say, as I don't think I moved beyond hoarding them. I managed an inch or so of curled, crusty Eucharists before a nosy neighbor, sitting in a pew behind us, informed my mother and she confiscated my jar. Through a misunderstanding of a phrase in our catechism, "the communion of saints," I transferred some of this magic to a pair of relics Nana kept on her bedroom dresser. Chips of bone encased in glass and metal, Nana's miniature reliquaries displayed the remains of Pope Pius X and another saint whose long name started with the letters *D-i-o-n* before fading into illegibility.

For years, I believed that smear of bone and glue *was* my dead aunt.

Everyone's idea of a Catholic childhood—sex, sin, guilt—infiltrated through the camouflage of the Catholic newspaper, the *Boston Pilot*. There were other double agents: Mary Magdalene particularly incited flustered conjecture whenever she turned up in our English reader. Each Saturday the *Pilot* printed the Legion of Decency List, a classification of current movies according to their "moral estimate." The infamous Class C—Condemned—probably was our earliest introduction to sex, certainly verbal sex. Along with now classic movies (from *Baby Doll* and *Never on Sunday* to *Jules and Jim*), the Condemned List chronicled stag films that played Boston's Combat Zone, no doubt salvaging numerous pulp-erotic titles from instant oblivion—*Port of Desire, Mating Urge, Question of Adultery, Love Game, The Molesters, Sins of Mona, Love Is My Profession,* or *Liane Jungle Goddess.* Condemned List movies, fascinatingly for us at St. Mark's, treated what looked like religious subjects: *Private Lives of Adam and Eve, Garden of Eden, Wages of Sin, And God Created Woman,* and—inevitably—*Magdalene.*

One of us chanced upon a stash of rain-soaked pornographic magazines during the walk home from school, and we raced them back to the St. Mark's playground. Fear spurred our excitement, and scads of confused jokes. But as we were divvying up the photographs for private study later, some older boys bullied the pages away, and started shredding. They left us a pile of tiny breasts and vaginas, each organ neatly ripped from its body, along with the taunting explanation we could hide these more easily from our parents.

By the time I reached the eighth grade, Nana was dead, and my family trailed white flight from Dorchester to suburban South Shore. After the Second Vatican Council, Mass was in English, with freshly translated Epistles and Gospels—and a folk Mass for the young people every Sunday morning. But we were listening to the Kinks, the Rolling Stones, Bob Dylan, and trying to look tough in sharkskin jackets that didn't quite tally with our red and gold school ties. The nuns at St. Ann's in Wollaston, here the Sisters of Charity of Nazareth, struggled to keep up. Instead of stories about Christ, the books at the back of our classroom carried titles like *Brass Knuckles,* and featured juvenile delinquents who renounced their gangs for the priesthood. The Reverend Walter J. Leach, Monsignor at St. Ann's, arranged a parish scholarship for me when I was accepted at Boston College High. But because of bureaucratic snags in the funding, he told my parents they should return to him $250 cash for each $500 check he wrote us. The scandal broke in the Boston papers long after I graduated. There were many parish scholars. Our kickbacks, among other church funds, found their way to a bank account in Sweden. The money was for the Swedish Missions, Monsignor Leach protested, before fleeing to Stockholm.

The one irruption of the Bible into B.C. High could not have looked more casual. We had just finished translating Book VI of the *Aeneid*, the descent of Aeneas into the underworld, and our Latin teacher decided to reward our efforts by introducing us to poems about hell. He read aloud a canto from Dante's *Inferno,* selections from Milton's *Paradise Lost,* the entire Old English "The Harrowing of Hell." You know, don't you, that in the Bible Jesus descends into hell? We didn't. He took up the last book from his pile, astonishingly—for us—the King James Bible, and read Matthew 12:38–45.

Matthew 12 opens with the hungry apostles foraging for food in a cornfield. When the Pharisees complain that "thy disciples do that which is not lawful to do on the sabbath day," Christ stirs to their defense:

> 3. But he said unto them, Have ye not read what David did, when he was an hungred, and they that were with him;

4. How he entered into the house of God, and did eat the shewbread, which was not lawful for him to eat, neither for them which were with him, but only for the priests?

5. Or have ye not read in the law, how that on the sabbath days the priests in the temple profane the sabbath, and are blameless?

6. But I say unto you, That in this place is *one* greater than the temple.

7. But if ye had known what *this* meaneth, I will have mercy, and not sacrifice, ye would not have condemned the guiltless.

8. For the Son of man is Lord even of the sabbath day.

Since we weren't used to hearing *any* Bible, except second hand through the catechism or condensed for Sunday Mass, no one spoke when our teacher asked us, what do you make of that? So he zeroed us in on the verbs and nouns, the grammar, the sounds of the old language, the way we pored over the *Aeneid*. The edgy, doubled questions ("Have ye not read . . . Or have ye not read"), the crisp, almost taunting subjunctive clause ("But if ye had known . . . ye would not have condemned"), and the blunt, crowning declaration ("For the Son of man is Lord . . .") declared *this* Christ another order of being from the genial Shepherd of our catechism, more classical, but more rock 'n' roll, too. Bold enough to arraign the priests' sanctimony against his disciples' hunger, and to summon King David as the forerunner of his own kingdom, Christ then proceeds directly into the Pharisees' synagogue. After the Pharisees accuse him of confederating with Beelzebub, Christ hones his rebuke:

25. And Jesus knew their thoughts, and said unto them, Every kingdom divided against itself is brought to desolation; and every city or house divided against itself shall not stand:

26. And if Satan cast out Satan, he is divided against himself; how shall then his kingdom stand?

27. And if I Beelzebub cast out devils, by whom do your children cast *them* out? therefore they shall be your judges.

28. But if I cast out devils by the Spirit of God, then the kingdom of God is come unto you.

29. Or else how can one enter into a strong man's house, and spoil his goods, except he first bind the strong man? and then he will spoil his house.

30. He that is not with me is against me; and he that gathereth not with me scattereth abroad.

Christ casts the riddle of his identity as an ascending ladder of logical drills: "If Satan . . . how shall then . . . "; "If I by Beelzebub . . . therefore . . ."; "But if I . . . by the spirit of God . . . then . . ." But his examples intimate a condemnation—the Pharisees, too, dwell in a "house divided against itself"—that stretches to a dire judgment, nearly a threat, or curse. "He that is not with me is against me." Informing the Pharisees that "by thy words thou shalt be justified, and by thy words thou shalt be condemned," Christ tags them "a generation of vipers." Beaten down, the Pharisees can think of nothing else but to request "a sign." Christ retorts with a gust of prophecy, his own harrowing of hell:

39. But he answered and said unto them, An evil and adulterous generation seeketh after a sign; and there shall no sign be given to it, but the sign of the prophet Jonas:

40. For as Jonas was three days and three nights in the whale's belly; so shall the Son of man be three days and three nights in the heart of the earth.

41. The men of Nineveh shall rise in judgment with this generation, and shall condemn it: because they repented at the preaching of Jonas; and behold, a greater than Jonas *is* here.

42. The queen of the south shall rise up in the judgment with his generation, and shall condemn it: for she came from the uttermost parts of the earth to hear the wisdom of Solomon; and, behold, a greater than Solomon *is* here.

43. When the unclean spirit is gone out of a man, he walketh through dry places, seeking rest, and findeth none.

44. Then he saith, I will return into my house from whence I came out; and when he is come, he findeth *it* empty, swept, and garnished.

45. Then goeth he, and taketh with himself seven other spirits more
    wicked than himself, and they enter in and dwell there: and the last
    state of that man is worse than the first. Even so shall it be also unto this
    wicked generation.

As Jonas fades to Christ, and the Old Testament jostles against, then blends into the New, horror drifts among the details—that weird "queen of the south," that spooky "last *state*"—much as a sad "unclean spirit" drifts "through dry places."

These were the words our Latin teacher put next to the *Aeneid*. His performance tilted the Bible into literature—not purified and negligible like the catechism, but Virgil, Dante, and Milton, strange, wondrous, difficult, terrifying. Perhaps sensing our shock, our excitement, he wound us down with some passages from Revelation, including—if I'm remembering right—Revelation 1:18:

> I *am* he that liveth, and was dead; and, behold, I am alive for evermore,
> Amen; and have the keys of hell and of death.

By then our class hour was over. His reading would not be repeated. I grew resourceful at not attending Mass, except for Christmas and Easter, and our family discussions of religion shifted to symbolic turf—the Vietnam War, long hair, Malcolm X, and what my father called garbage: rock music and most novels. My mother made sure our windows were shut for the neighbors as we fought at the dinner table, but did my father really believe what he was saying about Eugene McCarthy, antiwar protesters, the Beatles, drugs? Were his arguments another way for him to say he was American? I couldn't tell. I could see he stopped seeing me—from his vehemence you'd guess I was assembling bombs in our basement, or brewing acid. In Harvard Square I bought a used copy of Bertrand Russell's *Sceptical Essays* and debated whether to call myself an atheist or an agnostic. My mother would be troubled once she noticed I no longer went to church, my father sullen when I lost my interest in science.

After a French class spent translating Camus and Sartre, I stood trembling at my locker, sensing I was standing on nothing. But irony, glib though sometimes surprisingly sour, composed our main spiritual stance. Over the obligatory student applause and shouts that greeted the Jesuit hierarchy at B.C. High assemblies, my friends and I chanted, "Give us Barabbas!" "Give us Barabbas!" as proctors scurried to descry the source.

Our sneaky, feeble rebellion was itself, I suppose, homage to the New Testament we scarcely knew.

Confidential

She wears the Sacred Heart on her sleeve
for Christ's sake,
who would have pegged her as a blackmailer?

There is a photograph I used to live inside,
many have taken it one time or another—

By the end she would only step out
with her cute boy reporters,
the ones who wrote she was pretty, sad, & misunderstood—

Love came over us, everyone said, like destiny,
to give it up would be like giving up God—

But listen, this is confidential—

We are at the Formosa. It is no year
I can think of, but in rapid succession
I'm Frank Sinatra/
Barbara Stanwyck/ Gloria Graham/ Orson Welles.

You'd think this would be fun. They're all cool,
right? Plus all the sex,
the love, even? The yearning in those faces
yearning towards me. But it's not—

and not just because I have no control
over who I become—Orson/ Barbara/ Gloria/ Frank
. . . would it matter?

But instead I'm always too old—
or too young. Someone's just walked out on me,
or I've just left him or her.

I'm not discovered yet, or no one wants me
except for who I used to be.

I'm too drunk or too fat or too crazy.
I'm in someone's office, unzipping his fly.

I'm shouting—don't you know who I am!

And that's the problem, I always do.
I know exactly who I am.

Shooting Star

*"I seen a shooting star tonight,
and I thought of you . . . "*

In a San Francisco basement apartment
There's a woman I keep hearing about, who
Claims for the last twenty years she's lived
With Bob Dylan, and wishes to write a book about it.
That might mostly be new to him—*hey man,
You must be putting me on*. But she sells scarves
From her own North Beach shop, and according
To this woman Dylan's changed—a lot—
Heavy now, yet kind, if also a little
Crazy, in and out of hospitals, he doesn't look
Like himself. Still, wherever he travels
He mails her love poems in his familiar
'60s style, and she'd be honored to show them around.

A sleepy kitchen at dawn, the woman steps
Towards the kettle, pajamas open to her waist,
An owlish man, drunken, slothful, lags behind.
The glamour of the damaged, but how much
More gratifying for her not to have spun the whole
Hazy farrago out of loneliness, madness, or for money,
And this morning to wake beside someone
Who persuades you he recorded "Shooting Star" just for you.

Sister Elvis

I called myself Sister Elvis
                    until Memphis,

I called myself Sister Elvis
                    until the night I came

to in a blackout.

All my life I wanted to carry Elvis's face into the future—
Pretend to be filled with the Holy Spirit, everyone
said, *until you are.*

As far back as I can remember it was drizzling,
and I was dreaming Memphis in the rain as I wondered
what Elvis was doing.

The Lord gave Elvis to the world as a gift,
but when I sang you heard his voice.

That night in Memphis there was no moon, so throwing no
shadow I must have risen sick from the motel floor,

somehow I found my way to the bathroom mirror.
I took my car keys and cut and stabbed and cut at what I saw,

until Sister Elvis was just a dream and a lie.

2.

Are you lonesome tonight?

Elvis's body is in Graceland,
but his soul is in heaven,
and his spirit will always be here with us.

One time on the road, Elvis stopped
his car and got out.

"See that cloud?" he asked.
"I'm going to move that cloud."

And the cloud moved.

Maybe the wind blew it, I don't know.
Elvis, I'm told, only looked around

and smiled.

In this way his spirit guides me—
when I'm on stage Elvis takes over,
then I become his earthly vessel,

like a priest on Sunday
I'm giving the live performance,
because God himself can't be there in body—

believe me it takes a lot to stand before your congregation,
and pull something like that

out of your soul.

In high school the drama coach cast me as an intergalactic
female Elvis on a planet
ruled by women,

the smart fat boy who wrote the music believed
he was a girl,

song after song of ancient church music,
a slow, glorious drone.

Years later I heard the boy moved to San Francisco, raised
money enough to change his sex,
and came out as a lesbian.

I remember thinking that is an awfully roundabout way for
anyone to go,
just to sleep with girls. . . .

But who cared about *fucking* Elvis?
I wanted to be Elvis.

3.

Don't look at the guilt,
look at the blood.

All my men were cheap,
but they were quick,
my husband spoke little,
and only of sex,
and departed in somber haste after his seed was spent,

any Christian, he said, who would allow
any type of rock or country recording in her home,
she's inviting the powers of darkness;

any individual listening to it,
she's entering into communication with wickedness,
and evil spawned in hell.

But God called me,
from a Sears and Roebuck Gene Autry guitar—

You'll take my Gospel to the world.

The lights and the noise pulling me like a compass,
in a gold vest, my long hair slick with Brylcreem,
I ascended the stage of the county fair.

I grabbed the mic stand in my left hand,
hung my other arm over the guitar neck,
tipped back one shiny shoe,

and sneered a little laugh I saw him do—
Elvis became part of me that day.

Someone told me that at the premiere of *Love Me Tender*
when the character Elvis played was killed,
Gladys, Elvis's mother, started to cry,

but Elvis put his arm around her, said it was OK,
he was right there with her—

and on that cruel August morning I heard Elvis really did die,
I was afraid my voice would die too.

I knew that if I didn't pick up my guitar right away,
he would never sing again,

so I prayed I have sinned against you, my Lord,
and I would ask that your Precious Blood cleanse
all stain in the seas of God's forgetfulness,

and that morning God showed me his harvest fields.

4.

I think what God meant to say was,

Look at the blood—

No more tears,
the music, the beat takes over,
the audience and I seem to roll with it, as one—

Night after night—

Funny how you know what God means, then lose it,
then find and lose it all over again.

But when did I start to lose my way?
But right or wrong, wasn't the Elvis trail my way?

I prayed and drank, drank and prayed,
trying to make my days cancel my nights,
my nights canceling my days—

Until the night in Memphis,
a motel so close to Graceland,
coming to in a blackout of vodka and sin,

and I beg your forgiveness

what I can only call the awe of it all overcame me—
I took my keys and sacrificed the face of Sister Elvis,
offered my own face up to him.

My blood was everywhere—

I keep returning to that night,
the rain falling on Memphis
and coming to in a blackout

I cut and stabbed and cut,
and when I was done
I looked out the window at the silent cars, the motel signs,

there in the drops of rain and crud on the glass
the unmistakable likeness,
not my slashed face, but his,

his perfect cheekbones, forehead, nose looking
straight at me, so pretty, and I felt safe, overcome
no more, and I went outside to save all I could

of his image on a paper napkin—
my forever Shroud of Memphis.

Pacific Coast Highway

for R. H. 1999

As in the old story a man keeps crossing the street.
The first time his son is with him, stumbling
Ahead to the sidewalk behind their jeep,
Parked so they could watch it from the bar.
Just ahead railroad tracks, and beyond
Cottages, sand, the gray Pacific.
But each time the man crosses he is struck
By a black SUV, bounced onto the hood for 80 feet, and
Rolled another 50 down to the rail bed.
His son must be on the other side waiting.
Again, the man crosses the street.

Spicy Detective

Around that time I took to clipping and mailing in coupons from the advertisements I found at the back of old magazines for sale in junk stores.

Coupons for Exciting New Beauty in Three Minutes, Be a Radio Technician, How to Win at Contract Bridge, Bed Manners, I'll Send You This Handsome Sample Case Free, and Will You Spend $2 to Save Your Hair?

I always imagined the coupons going to the same spare, sunlit office—already a decade out of fashion by the date on the magazine—down a black-and-white tile corridor in the Empire State Building.

A suite there often was the actual address. A squat man in dark glasses and a wool vest, who reluctantly responds to the title "Chief," punches and files another coupon.

Riding with the King

You don't know about me, without

back when my name was Michael Edwards
I was the most successful male model across

Europe and the United States, I wrote
a book, my ghost did,
perhaps you remember me.

Perhaps you know my nightmare the first night
at Priscilla's—an enormous Elvis over the pool,
This is what it's like to be God, Elvis said.

Perhaps you know my next date with Priscilla,
Magic Mountain with Lisa Marie and her little friends,
I vomited the beer I drank behind the Spin of Death.

Perhaps you know I carried Priscilla past a pedestal
showing Elvis's gold-framed sunglasses with the big EP,
it was unsettling, I kicked the door shut behind us.

Perhaps you know I felt the stirrings of love
after our third bottle of wine when I over-
heard Priscilla random-dialing, impersonating a hooker.

Perhaps you know I came to see Priscilla was to Elvis
as Lisa Marie to me—after Elvis brought her to Memphis,
he put Priscilla in Catholic school,

Perhaps you know seeing Lisa looking
adorable in her wool skirt, white blouse, bobby
sox and loafers, I understood Elvis's feelings.

Perhaps you know in our acting class Priscilla
did a love scene, she and her partner went into a long kiss,
I knew exactly how Elvis felt, when he caught her.

Perhaps you know Lisa got up from the dinner table
to go to the refrigerator, her bare knee
brushed my hand.

Perhaps you know I was in a mood for some photos,
I dressed Lisa in her mother's vintage gowns,
her eyes and lips replicas of Elvis's.

Perhaps you know I put an end to swimming
together when Lisa threw her arms around me, we bounced
up and down, I became aroused.

Perhaps you know Priscilla and I returned
after an argument about my drinking,
she went to her bathroom, I went into Lisa's room.

Perhaps you know I wanted someone to talk to,
but Lisa was asleep.

Perhaps you know I lifted a corner of the covers,
and gazed at her.

Perhaps you know I woke with a hangover,
alone in bed.

Perhaps you know Priscilla and I were secretive about
our fighting.

Perhaps you know Priscilla and Elvis were the same,
until his staff exposed them in *Elvis — What Happened?*

Perhaps you know driving home through Los Angeles,
I felt numb,

Perhaps you know every car I looked in,
I saw happy couples,

Perhaps you know as I waited for the light to change,
I thought of the three of us.

You don't know about me without you have read
a book by the name of *Priscilla, Elvis and Me*,

that book was made by Michael Edwards,
he mainly told the truth.

The Great Awakening

Oh, de wars and de scrapes
And de sprees am done — sprees am done
De foe am beat.
De Turks am drowned — Turks am drowned.
All safe and sound
To our wives we come . . .
— *Otello*, BY T. D. RICE

Dreams may come from the enemy—

from the business of the past day—

from a disordered body—

from moral evil—

from God,

through the medium of the Angels, and departed saints, as forewarnings to stir up and
prepare the mind for the scenes ahead.

    I fell into a slumber; and in it I dreamed that two devils entered the room, each
with a chain in his hand; they laid hold on me, the one at my head, the other at my
feet, and bound me fast, and breaking out the window, carried me a distance from the
house and laid me on a spot of ice, and while the weaker devil flew off in flames of fire,
the stronger one set out to carry me down to hell.

    I put my hands together and said, Lord I submit to go and preach thy gospel; only
grant my peaceful hours to return, and open the door.

    Here I received the solemn news of the death of our only child.

The vibration of the earth shook down the trees, thousands of willows were swept off like a pipe stem, about waist high, and the swamps became high ground, and high land became low ground, and two islands in the river were so shaken, washed away and sunk, as not to be found.

From this I infer some trouble is at hand,
But the film was already starting—

The sounds came in waves, higher
and higher, at the top of it
someone screaming—

Now what you call your great disappointment,
I call the Great Awakening—

When I heard (though not always
in these old forgotten words I remember) the first of three visions—

Yet if you tell me they are only
my dear dead returning,
I would not disbelieve you.

2.

It is an odd sort of fortune to have lived an adventurous life.

In my disgust, I left school and devoted
all my blighted spirit to minstrelsy;
I had no natural aptness for the banjo,
but for dancing—
such a remarkable gift few ever saw.

The first part of our performances
we gave with white faces;
and by practicing to knock spin and toss the tambourine
back in my room,
I was now the "Scotch Girl" in plaid petticoats.

Besides my Highland Fling, I took the principal lady parts
in the negro ballets;
for a lad, I danced "Lucy Long" so admirably
a planter in one of the Southern States insisted on purchasing me,
until the door-tender kicked that planter down the stairs.

Old Ephraim was one of the most comical specimens
of the negro species,
the blackest face, largest mouth, whitest teeth;
What could he do?
Why, he could fetch water, black our boots, take care of our baggage.

My father said of Howie Gray
who worked beside him every day at the South Station PO
and put both his sons through college,
"He's not an uppity Negro."
My father meant that as a compliment.

There were tears in his eyes when Howie Gray died.

3.

Every man his own radio—

It hath been thought that the dying speeches of such as have been executed among us
might be of singular use to correct the crimes wherein too many do live

Billington, disregarding the commotion he was causing and the certainty of apprehension, reloaded and stalked his enemy.

She concealed her crime until the time of her delivery, and then being delivered alone by her self in a dark room, she murdered the harmless and helpless infant.

Foster didn't say a word. He just picked up a steal boomer and smashed Pikin over the head with it.

I went forth to be delivered in the field, and dropping my child by the side of a little pond (whether alive or stillborn I cannot tell), I covered it over with dirt and snow and speedily returned home.

He struck the helpless Kling again and again.

Mr. Spooner strove to speak, when down, Brooks took him by the throat and partly strangled him. Ross and Buchanan came out. Ross took Mr. Spooner's watch and gave it to Buchanan. Brooks and Ross took him up and put him in the well head first. Before they carried him away, I, Buchanan, pulled off his shoes.

Eight streaks of splattered blood. Eight murderous strokes of an axe or knife.

Was found, by a person with a dog, crossing the fields, in a piece of woods a little distance from Brandywine to the Turk's Head, two dead infants.

Now what you call your Great Awakening,
I call *Much Ado*,
I call *The Big Sleep*—

But when did I become someone on whom
everything is lost?

Like the dream I lifted from my father like a Band-Aid—

Where I checked hats,
that instantly, embarrassingly disappeared—

My earnest offers to return the $1.00 gratuity
raining down on dead ears—

I thought I was boyish.
It availed me nothing.

Last Seen

I remember my father strapped to the bed, repeating "God-Oh-God," the only other sound the ping of the life support.

I remember Mark climbing up into his blue truck for the drive back to Marion.

I remember stopping at the door, and waving to my mother. She would be released from the hospital on Monday.

I remember Arthur at my mother's funeral, an oxygen canister beside him in the aisle of the church.

I remember listening to Mark talk about his book—a chapter on each of his ten favorite songs, including Elvis Costello's "King Horse"—and the lesions on his tongue, his joke about the coincidence of his drugstore canker medicine, Cank-aid, and AIDS.

I remember thinking how tired he looked, as I put Jimmy into a cab outside the movie theater where we had just seen *Vanya on 42nd Street*.

I remember Elvis trying to stand and greet Dr. Russo.

* * *

There are terrible spirits, ghosts, in the air of America, D. H. Lawrence wrote in 1923.

I thought of Lawrence's ghosts often those early days after the towers came down, particularly when the flyers of the missing—always "the missing"—started to cover lower Manhattan, most spectacularly throughout Union Square, but also on nearly every wall, storefront, telephone booth, lamp pole, and tree south of 14th Street. Some of the flyers were plain as a wanted poster—a black-and-white photograph; minimal docket of vital statistics. But the images on the flyers of the missing usually were in color, and caught the loved one during passages of conspicuous happiness —a wedding, graduation, or party—and attired in celebratory, often formal dress, tuxedos and gowns. Many cradled babies in their arms. And nearly all carried a prominent scar, mole, tattoo: *5'11" 184 lbs. Blue Eyes Tattoo of Bulldog on Shoulder Last Seen 1 WTC 102 Floor Please Contact. . . .*

You needed to imagine a legion of the missing—5,000 those first weeks— wandering New York, lost, amnesiac, waiting for someone to recognize them from their photo and life story, and send them home. *Those that are pushed out of life in chagrin,* Lawrence continued, *come back unappeased, for revenge.*

* * *

A beautiful fall morning, perhaps still more beautiful because of the quiet. During the brief space between the moments the planes hit and the towers fell, I kept running down to the street to stare again at the flames, twenty blocks away, as if to prove this wasn't a TV spectacle. Sixth Avenue was a scene from a monster movie—hundreds of silent men and women moving uptown, all of them walking unnaturally fast, or unnaturally slow, craning their heads back over their shoulders for another look.

Hollywood & God

If only God would save me,
I would know how to hurt you.

If only God would save me,
I would know who to sell my soul to.

Anything is an autobiography,
but this is a conversation—

William Burroughs insisted
literature lagged 50 years behind painting,

thinking no doubt about abstraction, collage,
fragmentation, his cut-ups.

But whatever that meant (why always 50 years?), or however
he presumed to rile other writers,

poetry probably does lag behind any credible media theory about it—

so that if I put a pine tree
into a poem,

a grove of pine trees
and beyond them the sea,

you'd think it was the same tree Wordsworth put there;
instead of two obligatory centuries of nature studies, all those

Technicolor vistas, torch songs, couples
drifting through leaves in Salem commercials.

Into one life and out another,

the way a junkie playing a writer,
a writer playing a priest,

so that when I finally blurted out,
You-betrayed-me / I-wounded-you / We're-so-unhappy

you assumed the burden of personal urgency,
supposed it was me speaking at the limits of my self-control

and not *The Damned Don't Cry*,
Temptation, and *Leave Her to Heaven*.

You open your mouth and a tradition dribbles out.

But that's mimesis—

how almost impossible to avoid mimesis,
anybody's hardest truths prompting the most fractured constructions,

the way to think about God might be
to disobey God,

if only God's wish to remain hidden,

so that if everything is an autobiography,
this is a conversion.

As my lives flash before me,

why must the yearning for God
trump all other yearnings?

You often hear converts confess
the drinking, his pills, her sexual addiction,

concealed inside them a yearning for God—
why not the other way around?

The admission of Jesus into your life
concealing instead the wish, say, a need

to be fucked senseless drunk drugged & screaming
OH GOD! OH GOD! on a hotel bed . . .

God embraces our yearnings.

That afternoon my father heard his diagnosis of inoperable cancer,
my aunt Barbara demanded we get him to Lourdes.

She demanded this with a glass of vodka in her hand—
she demanded this running her fingers up and down my leg—
she demanded this before she passed out in her car—

In the movie of my life,
my father died

after I forgave him,

& when my secret tormentor said may the ghosts of your dreams
gnaw at your belly like a wolf under your jacket,

did she really want revenge,
or was she just killing time?

For me God is a hair shirt, or he's nothing;
for me God is a pain in the ass;

that's mimesis, again,

this hour I tell you things in confidence,
I might not tell everybody, but I'll tell you.

The world is a road under the wall to the church,
the world is a church, & the world is a road,

& the world is a stone wall.

Still, he wanted her the way the Cardinal wanted the Caravaggio,
& when the ill-advised possessor of the painting resisted—
one night Papal Guards searched his house.

Of course contraband came to light, some illegal rifles,
& when the ill-advised possessor of the painting went to prison—
the Cardinal got his Caravaggio.

But I wasn't a Cardinal, nephew to the Pope,
and you—
you were not a Caravaggio.

So I asked you to be in my movie.

Shame

This all started with a photograph I saw perhaps once and never again. We were packing up our old house in Dorchester—the first-floor flat of a classic Boston three-decker that Nana, my mother's mother, owned on Semont Road—for our move to Quincy. I had been taken by my father on a Saturday afternoon not long before to look over the new house, our first single-family home, on Hillside Avenue, appropriately near the summit of a minor hill. (The next street up was Summit Avenue.) The place was a wreck, the living room ceiling cracked and at the center dipping perilously, holes as though punched in the walls, bathtub dripping mold. But there were fine compensatory curiosities: a clapboard toolshed out back, a huge skull-shaped rock next to a stone fireplace for burning leaves, oak and fir trees, domed bushes for hiding. Inside off the front entrance hall was the smallest bathroom I've ever seen—even at age seven I could barely sit down without my knees hitting the pipes under the tiny sink. And I would finally have my own room—no longer sharing with Nana, as in Dorchester, the original master bedroom over the street, sleeping side by side in twin beds like a couple from a 1940s Hollywood movie. Whenever I was angry at my parents I would find the printed cardboard sign we used to signal that we needed heating oil and shove it in our bedroom bay window for the silver trucks that prowled the neighborhood, confusion and shouts at the door after a delivery man refilled our tank in summer or topped us off for the third time that winter week.

This would have been late in 1960—my first Quincy memory is watching the Kennedy inauguration on a TV that my father set up for us in the basement while workers plastered and painted upstairs. But while moving from Dorchester I was helping my father empty his dresser into cartons for the movers—his white work shirts and sleeveless T-shirts, his black sox, his boxer shorts—saving the top drawer, his junk drawer, for last.

I always liked to look through his dresser if there was no one home, or just me and my younger sister and brother. All sorts of objects might spill out of the cigar boxes and trays in his junk drawer. Old coins, some inserted into blue folders, lots of stamps (he worked for the post office), his World War II medals and pins, a few $25 US Savings Bonds with my name on them—for college, he said—and lots of shiny silver shoehorns (weekends he moonlighted downtown at a woman's shoe store). Mornings after he took my mother out for dinner and dancing—maybe once every other month on a Friday night, occasionally to Boston nightclubs with names like the High Hat, more often to VFW posts and church functions—there would be a fresh pack of smokes in his top drawer, always filtered, mostly Kents, with just two or three cigarettes missing. As far as I could see he never retrieved the old pack the next time they went out. So the Kents tended to pile up, and my parents must have smoked as they drank, taking years to drain the bottle of Seagram's 7 they stored in a dining room hutch for guests.

In his junk drawer my father kept a locked metal box, though "locked" and "metal" significantly embellish its dime-store, chipped and battered flimsiness. Still, it resisted all my attempts to pick it with a screwdriver and tweezers. But on this day that we were moving, he opened the box right up with a little key that apparently was inside the drawer all along, undetected by me, and out came everything you'd expect someone like my father should consider valuable or at risk—his service discharge papers, his and my mother's Social Security cards, their marriage license, our birth certificates, a red bank book from a decade earlier, and the ring he fashioned during the war for my mother out of a seashell and a New Guinea coin. I can recall all of this because the box came to me, contents more or less intact, after my father died. I keep the mother-of-pearl ring in a dish on a windowsill with both of my parents' wedding rings.

On this day there were photos in the box too, my parents seated by themselves at a table in a dining room I didn't recognize, some soldiers in uniform, young and smiling, my father among them, then what looked like two really ancient photos made—it seemed to me—from the same black metal as the box that held them, individual photos of a man with a mustache and a woman. Though the woman's picture was on top, my father quickly slipped it under the other one of the man like he was shuffling cards, and said that's your grandfather. Since I found out later that my grandfather died when I was four, less than three years before, presumably I met him. This is the only likeness I have of him. That thin mustache. A dark man in a dark suit and dark hat. Looking incredibly uncomfortable, like he never wore suits, or just didn't want to be there.

Of course my Irish grandmother, Nana, was still alive, and there were photographs of her family everywhere in the Dorchester house—her parents, sisters and brothers, her dead husband, her two other children, my Aunt Mary and Uncle John, both also dead, from cancer before they turned forty. But this Italian grandfather doesn't turn up even among the hundreds of snapshots in my parents' wedding album. I must have asked my father about the woman in the first photo, the dark girl who looked to be (I would say now) in her teens. I understood right away without being told or knowing why, beyond their same beak-like nose and large black eyes, that she was connected to my father, the way you usually know when someone is about to betray you or hurt you, even though there aren't any obvious signs and warnings, you feel it along your skin. Orphans fascinated me and part of my Dad's particular fascination for me was that he had lost his mother when he was around my age, was on his own from the age of five, his father always away working. He said he had only one memory of his mother: he was playing in the kitchen, swinging on the door of their icebox, when the whole thing toppled over on him. His mother called out the window for help, and when nobody came she lifted off the icebox herself, even though she was a small woman and frail, perhaps already dying. He told me just one story about his father too, laughing and shaking his head as he talked: he said that my dockworker grandfather, Luigi Polito, was among the thousands of stupid Bostonians who in 1920 rushed down to 27 School Street to invest their wages in Charles Ponzi's Securities Exchange Company.

I can't remember what I thought my father meant by a "Ponzi scheme," or even if he told me about Ponzi then or later. I'm guessing that he was trying to distract me from the photograph of the woman—distract me as people will do when they're agitated, as my father visibly was then—by discussing *technique*. We discussed technique a lot. Does that mean we were often agitated? For most of my childhood my father was in many ways my closest friend. A friendship of common interests, like science, rockets, UFOs, and gadgets. Then we got very competitive. He told me that long ago photographs were first made of glass and then they were made of tin. His information mostly was wrong of course—or I got it wrong: daguerreotypes aren't printed on glass; the glass only protects the fragile plates. Tintypes aren't tin at all but thin iron sheets. But tintypes were popular with street photographers into the 1930s, for neighborhood fairs and carnivals. Did my father's tintypes come from one of the Italian summer street fairs—the St. Anthony Festival? St. Rocco?—in Boston's North End?

In the tintype the woman I've always assumed is my grandmother stands on the arc of a little bridge, holding a flower. There was no water under the bridge, so this must have been a set in an impromptu photography studio. A curtain backdrop, I think, also provided trees, plus the moon and the outline of a distant river. The woman wore an elaborate dress imprinted with leaves and flowers, and a kind of cape over the dress. There were also flowers and leaves in her hair, which appeared black and curly like my father's and flowed along her shoulders into the swirls of her cape and dress. Her mouth open, smiling almost, she gazes at the camera, or the cameraman, or someone standing behind him, or whoever happens to be looking back at her image.

Later over the years when I mentioned these photos, my father always denied their existence. He said he had no photographs of his mother, and his sister, my Aunt Ann, kept the few pictures there were of my grandfather. My grandfather was an Italian peasant, he said, who didn't like cameras and photographs. He unloaded fish from ships in Boston harbor for the big seafood restaurants. He even tried to force my father to leave school and join him on the docks. He was a laborer. He never wore a suit.

My mentioning the photographs became a funny family story, something like the time I went on a deep-sea fishing trip with my father and supposedly caught thirty-six fish. To my eventual humiliation it actually was the charter-boat captain who caught all the fish; he just handed me the fishing rod whenever he felt a tug on the line. Or the time that my fever spiked to 105 degrees and, as my father recalled, I went off my rocker, babbling delirious about God knows what. These photos were yet another instance of me going off my rocker.

I never saw that photograph of my grandmother again. No tintypes at all were in the metal box by the next time my sister and I opened it some thirty-five years later, after my mother died and more than a decade after the death of my father. But as I say, nearly everything else was there, all the papers, the shell ring, the other snapshots— though, oddly, the photograph of my grandfather wasn't a tintype either but a photographic postcard. Still, my father told me about tintypes that day we moved, so the photo of the dark, curly-haired woman must have been a tintype. From other tintypes and cabinet cards I've seen since, I realize the woman looked like, or was trying to look like, an opera singer, or an actress.

Once my mother died, I learned more from my sister about my grandmother. This was the way my father apparently told it to my mother who then told it to her. Around 1914 my grandfather arrived in the United States from Naples with his wife and their two children, George and Ann. His wife soon after was very ill and returned to Italy, taking the children home with her. A few years later she died, and George and Ann started to grow up with relatives on a vineyard near Bari. My father meanwhile was born in Boston in 1915, to a woman who appears as "Angela DiRuggiero" on his birth certificate and as "Mary Ruggiero" on his wedding license. There's no evidence that she and my grandfather were married then, or any time later. Angela, or Mary, didn't die when my father was five; instead she left my grandfather, my father, and Boston for New York City. My grandfather summoned George and Ann from Italy, and Ann raised my father, who never saw his mother again.

Because this was a mother abandoning a child, I've always assumed there must have been another man involved. But who knows? Apparently my grandfather was a drunk, and so abusive and violent that he wasn't allowed to attend my parents' wedding. After I got to high school, my father and I fought about the war in Vietnam, Nixon, rock music, and my wanting to be an English professor and not an engineer. Nights when I came in the back door and passed him on the porch with his bound books of *New York Times* crossword puzzles, I thought he looked like the unhappiest person I'd ever met.

Now I don't think *unhappy* so much as ashamed. Something of the world my father must have lived inside, on the porch with his puzzles, hit me the one time I attempted to find out what happened to my grandmother from my Auntie Ann. "Your father was a good man, Bobby," she snapped back, as though this was the only possible answer to my question, and shut the subject down.

I've looked for that tintype ever since, and nearly any weekend in upstate New York I will find one at some antique store, usually for a few dollars, but occasionally a lot more if it's tinted or the store is posh. A dealer who gets them for me says that locals will sell old photographs to him even when they know the portraits are from their own family, and he offers practically nothing for them. I never met these people, they tell him. So sometimes I can buy multiple pictures of the same person, and groups who are clearly related, the tintypes still tucked into their original books, though damaged by water and insects.

I make my living writing about art, and have friends who collect what they call vernacular photography. But this has nothing to do with art. More like I'm assembling an alternate family, the way a childless couple might gather cats and dogs around them. I have stacks of the tintypes now, all over the place. When I see a photograph of a young woman with dark hair who would have been alive in 1915, posed against some fantastic contrived scene, I pay whatever it costs. Then I start looking for her all over again.

Notes

These poems reflect and absorb many sources, a few to a full mash-up, collaged, or even found degree, others incidental, some obvious, some probably not. I was occasionally aiming for collective as well as personal utterance, and along with perhaps inevitable citations and adaptations (Whitman, Stein, Pessoa, *The Killing*, Jim Thomson, Sam Fuller, Twain), you will also hear Cotton Mather, some eighteenth-century execution sermons and last-speech broadsides (Mary Martin, Esther Rodgers, James Buchanan, Elizabeth Wilson), early criminal autobiographies (especially Henry Tufts), Lorenzo Dow's *History of Cosmopolite* (1848), Ralph Keeler's *Vagabond Adventures* (1870), Manny Farber, Nick Tosches, David Goodis, Janice Kucera, and Rob Brezsny, among others. My debt and gratitude to these writers, and also to the authors of the books and films named and acknowledged inside the poems themselves.